A New True Book

SOUTH AMERICA

By D.V. Georges

CHILDRENS PRESS ®

CHICAGO

Brazilian carnival costume

PHOTO CREDITS

© Cameramann International, Ltd.—2, 27, 34 (2 photos), 35 (left), 40 (left), 41, 43 (bottom right), 44 (left)

Gartman Agency:
© Susan Malis—16 (left), 43 (top left), 43 (top right)
© Zaloudek—17 (left)

Journalism Services: © Mark Gamba—38 (bottom left), 43 (bottom left)

Photri—12 (right), 17 (right), 19 (left), 33 (left), 37 (left)

R/C Agency: © Richard L. Capps—13 (left), 14 (left)

© H. Armstrong Roberts:
29 (bottom left), 38 (top left), 44 (right)
© Nadine Orabona—23 (left)
© Puttkamer/ZEFA—21 (left)
© K. Scholz—13 (right)
© Maurice Rosalsky—38 (bottom right)

Tom Stack & Associates:
© Rod Allin—16 (right)
© John Cancalosi—18
© George D. Dodge—22
© Warren Garst—23 (right)
© Gary Milburn—12 (center), 24 (left), 26 (right), 38 (top right), 40 (right), 42
© M. Timothy O'Keefe—21 (right)
© Don Rutledge—29 (top left)

Valan Photos:
© Kennon Cooke—24 (right)
© Herman H. Giethoorn—25 (left)
© Jean-Marie Jro—Cover, 14 (right), 15 (left), 29 (bottom right), 30 (right), 31, 35 (right)
© Sylvain Majeau—25 (right)
© Robert C. Simpson—26 (left)

Maps—Albert R. Magnus, 4, 6, 8, 10, 12, 15, 19, 29, 30, 33, 37, 45

Cover—Llama grazing on the altiplano

Library of Congress Cataloging-in-Publication Data

Georges, D.V.
    South America.

    (A New true book)
    Includes index.
    Summary: Discusses characteristics of various sections of South America such as the Andes, the Amazon rain forest, and the pampas.
    1. South America—Juvenile literature. [1. South America—Geography]   I. Title.
    F2208.5.G46 1986   918   86-9584
    ISBN 0-516-01296-7

TABLE OF CONTENTS

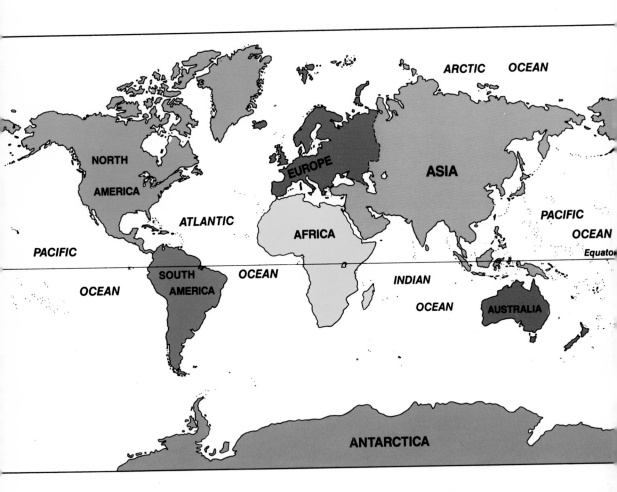

ARCTIC OCEAN

NORTH
AMERICA

EUROPE

ASIA

PACIFIC
OCEAN

ATLANTIC

AFRICA

PACIFIC

OCEAN

Equator

OCEAN

SOUTH
AMERICA

INDIAN

AUSTRALIA

OCEAN

OCEAN

ANTARCTICA

FINDING SOUTH AMERICA

A continent is a great area of land. There are seven continents in the world. They are Asia, Africa, North America, South America, Antarctica, Europe, and Australia.

South America is the fourth-largest continent. It is two thirds the size of its neighbor, North America. The Isthmus of Panama connects South America to

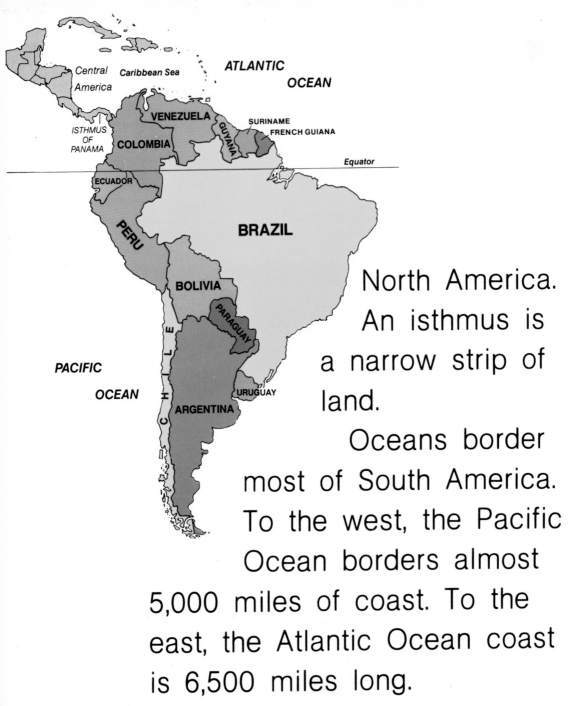

North America. An isthmus is a narrow strip of land.

Oceans border most of South America. To the west, the Pacific Ocean borders almost 5,000 miles of coast. To the east, the Atlantic Ocean coast is 6,500 miles long.

SPAIN AND PORTUGAL IN SOUTH AMERICA

In 1498, Christopher Columbus made his third voyage from Spain to the West Indies. When he touched the shores of Venezuela he became the first explorer to land in South America.

The next year, Amerigo Vespucci also sailed from Spain to Venezuela. From there he traveled east and

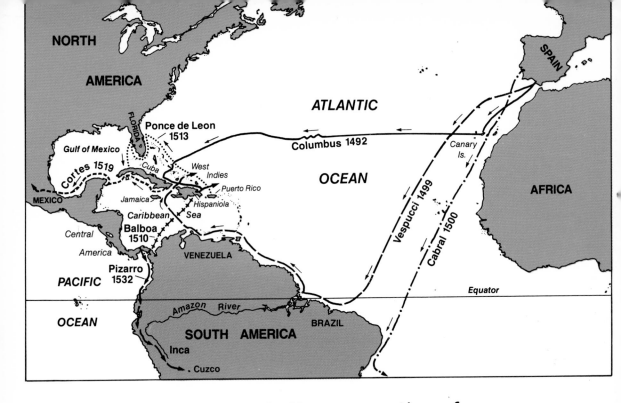

discovered the mouth of
the Amazon River. South
America and North
America are named for
Amerigo Vespucci.

In 1500, the navigator
Pedro Alvares Cabral
claimed Brazil for Portugal.

Brazil covered one third of South America. But Spain conquered much of the rest of the continent. The Spanish conquerers were called conquistadors.

Francisco Pizarro was one of the most famous conquistadors. In 1532, he defeated the great Inca Empire.

The French, Dutch, and British founded settlements in South America between Venezuela and Brazil. They

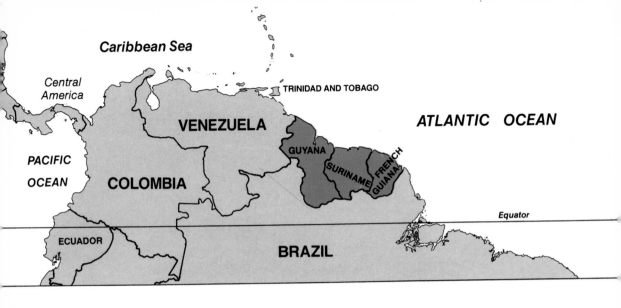

were much smaller than lands claimed by Spain and Portugal.

The settlement that was British is now the country of Guyana. The Dutch settlement became the country of Suriname. The French settlement is called French Guiana.

THE ANDES

The Andes form the longest mountain chain in the world. They follow the entire west coast of South America, from Venezuela to the southern tip of the continent.

The highest peak in the Western Hemisphere is in the Andes. It is Mount Aconcagua, in Argentina. Mount Aconcagua is more than four miles high.

The Andes Mountains

Andean condor at close range and in flight

Andean condors soar
through the high peaks.
The wingspan of Andean
condors is ten feet. They
are the largest flying birds.

In the Andes lives the
small spectacled bear. It is
the only South American
bear. White marks around
its eyes look like glasses.

Spectacled bears (left) are disappearing as highways through the Andes Mountains (right) invade their living areas.

Few mountains in the world have as many steep-sided canyons and wide plateaus as the Andes. Rivers have cut through rock to form the deep canyons.

Plateaus are high flatlands. The largest plateau of the Andes is

13

Bird's eye view of the altiplano (left). Crossing Lake Titicaca (right)

the altiplano. It is the size of New York State. Most of the altiplano is in western Bolivia. Part of it is in Peru.

On the altiplano, Lake Titicaca lies between Peru and Bolivia. La Paz—the capital of Bolivia—is near the eastern shore of Lake Titicaca. La Paz is the highest capital in the world.

The city of La Paz, Bolivia

ECUADOR

PERU

BRAZIL

Cuzco

Lake
Titicaca

La Paz

BOLIVIA

PARAGUAY

CHILE

ARGENTINA

The Altiplano

more than two miles above
sea level!

Hundreds of years ago,
the plateaus and valleys of
Bolivia, Peru, and Ecuador
were part of the great Inca
Empire. Cuzco, in Peru,
was the capital.

Machu Picchu (left) and Cuzco (right) are Inca cities.

In 1911, ruins of an Inca city were discovered at Machu Picchu. Machu Picchu is not far from Cuzco. But it is high up on a small, hidden plateau. Because the plateau was not flat, the Incas built terraces and steps throughout the city.

Many people who live in

Llamas (left) are related to the camel. Copper mine (above) in Chile

the Andes have small farms. They grow potatoes, corn, and fruit. Often they also raise llamas or alpacas.

Some people work in mines. There are silver mines in Bolivia and Peru, copper mines in Chile, and gold mines in Colombia.

THE AMAZON RAIN FOREST

The Amazon rain forest covers one third of South America. It is a region of heavy rainfall and high temperatures.

The rain forest begins east of the Andes of Colombia, Ecuador, Peru, and Bolivia. From these

The muddy Amazon River

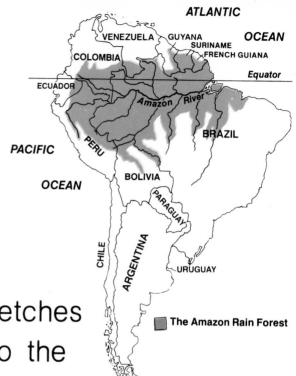
The Amazon Rain Forest

countries it stretches across Brazil to the Atlantic.

The Amazon River flows through the rain forest. Its source is in the Andes of Peru. It flows east four thousand miles and empties into the Atlantic Ocean. Because of the high rainfall there are many rivers in the rain forest. The Amazon River has five hundred tributaries!

In northeastern Brazil, the mouth of the Amazon River crosses the equator.

Trees grow tall in the rain forest. In Brazil, timber from mahogany and cedar trees is an important industry. Rubber trees and Brazil nut trees are also important.

Workers (left) cut down trees at Mato Grosso.
A Yagua hut (right) in the Amazon rain forest.

To serve the timber industry, towns have been built on the Amazon River and its tributaries. Deep in the rain forest, however, there are few towns.

In remote parts of the forest live Indian groups.

Yagua Indians practicing with blow pipes

The Indians hunt forest animals. They have small farms where they grow cassava. Bread is made from the roots of the cassava plant.

The rain forest is full of unusual animals. Many of the animals live in the trees. Sloths hang upside

Uakari monkey   Two-toed sloth

down from tree branches.
They walk, eat, and even
sleep upside down!

Uakaris and marmosets
are small monkeys of the
Amazon. Uakaris live very
high in the trees. Indians
have them as pets. People
catch marmosets and sell
them in other countries as

A golden lion marmoset (left) and
a family of spider monkeys (above)

pets. The pygmy marmoset
is only six inches long.
The golden lion marmoset
has soft yellow fur.

Spider monkeys are
much larger. They have very
long arms and a long tail.

Scarlet macaws (left) and a
brightly colored toucan (above)

Macaws are large
parrots of the rain forest.
Toucans are relatives of
woodpeckers. They have
big, brightly colored beaks.

Some dangerous animals
also live in the Amazon
rain forest. The anaconda
is a giant snake. It can be

Yellow anaconda (above)
Piranha (right)

eight yards long and a
foot thick! It is a
constrictor snake—it
strangles its prey.

The piranha is a fish of
the river waters. It is not
large, but it has razor-
sharp teeth. Piranhas feed
on animals, including
people.

HIGHLANDS OF BRAZIL

In Brazil, highlands rise up south of the rain forest. The highlands cover nearly half of the country.

Coffee is an important crop of the highlands. Seeds of the coffee tree are roasted and ground to make coffee. Brazil produces more coffee than any other country.

Major cities of Brazil are in the highlands. São Paulo and Rio de Janeiro are ports on the Atlantic. Hills of the highlands are a scenic backdrop for the cities.

Rio de Janeiro used to be the capital of Brazil. In 1960, Brasília became the capital. Unlike most cities, Brasília was completely planned. Architects planned all the streets and

Tourists like to visit the modern cities of
São Paulo (top left), Rio de Janeiro (bottom
left), and Brasília (bottom right).

From the air, Brasília is
a city of lovely designs.

buildings. Streets of
downtown Brasília are laid
out in the shape of an
airplane!

The southern tip of Brazil
borders Paraguay, Uruguay,
and Argentina. The Iguaçu
River forms part of the

Iguaçu Falls

border between Brazil and Argentina. It is a tributary of the great Paraná River. Near where the two rivers meet are the famous Iguaçu Falls. The spectacular falls spread over a mile-wide area.

PAMPAS

Pampas are the fertile flatlands of northeast Argentina. They are covered with farms and ranches. Wheat and beef from the pampas are exported to many other countries.

The Paraná River flows through the pampas. It is the second-largest river in South America. Only the Amazon River is larger.

The Paraná River

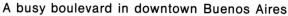
A busy boulevard in downtown Buenos Aires

empties into Río de la Plata, a large inlet of the Atlantic Ocean. Buenos Aires—the capital of Argentina—is on Río de la Plata. Buenos Aires is a scenic city and an important port.

Buenos Aires is a leading exporter of beef.

Trains link remote parts of the pampas. The trains carry products from farms and ranches to Buenos Aires. Many of the products are then shipped out of the port.

Less rain falls in the western part of the pampas.

The Argentine cowboy (left) is called
a gaucho. Oil mining (above) is an
important industry.

The very dry Gran Chaco
region borders the pampas
far to the west. It extends
into Paraguay.

Most of the people in
the Gran Chaco raise
cattle. There are also oil
fields in the region.

AT THE SOUTHERN TIP OF SOUTH AMERICA

The southern part of South America is cone shaped. Within the cone is Patagonia, the barren flatland of Argentina. West of Patagonia are the Andes. The Atlantic Ocean is to the east.

East and west meet at the islands of Tierra del Fuego. They are at the southern tip of South America.

The vast plains of Tierra del Fuego

PERU

BOLIVIA

BRAZIL

PARAGUAY

PACIFIC
OCEAN

CHILE

ARGENTINA

URUGUAY

ATLANTIC
OCEAN

PATAGONIA

Strait of Magellan
Tierra del Fuego

The Strait of Magellan separates Tierra del Fuego from the rest of South America. The strait is named for Ferdinand Magellan. In 1520, Magellan discovered Tierra del Fuego and sailed

37

Ferdinand Magellan (top left) sailed through the Strait of Magellan (bottom right), just south of the region called Patagonia (top right). Both the strait and the penguins (bottom left) living near the strait were named after him.

through the strait. He led the first expedition to sail around the world. The expedition was successful, but Magellan died before it was completed.

The climate of Tierra del Fuego can be cold. In Spanish, Tierra del Fuego means "land of fire." Explorers called it this because of the fires the native people built. At night, Tierra del Fuego appeared to be on fire.

The future of South America lies in the contributions of the young as well as the old.

SOUTH AMERICA'S FUTURE

The countries of South America have much in common. Most of the people speak Spanish. In Brazil, people speak Portuguese.

Aerial view of Caracas, the capital of Venezuela

In most South American countries, the capital cities are centers for industry, banking, and trade. There are many modern buildings. Often they stand just blocks from historic sites.

Sellers bring their daily produce to a street market.

But outside the large cities, the way of life is not yet modern. Most people work on farms near small villages. On the smaller farms, few machines are used. Farmers still do much of the work by hand.

Change is coming slowly to the villages of South

Large-scale farming (top left) is done with modern machinery (bottom right). However, in small villages farmers still use oxen (top right) to plow their land. Some still separate wheat by hand (bottom left).

Today, workers in modern cities put
up with rush-hour traffic (right)
to work as technicians (above) in industrial jobs.

America. To reach and
educate people takes a
long time, especially in
remote places.

South America is rich in
minerals and oil fields. Its
countries are just starting
to become modern nations.
They have much to look
forward to.

WORDS YOU SHOULD KNOW

architect(AR • kih • tekt)—a person who designs buildings

cassava(ka • SAH • va)—a plant of the tropics whose roots are used to make bread

conquistadors(kon • KEE • sta • dorz)—Spanish conquerors

empire(EM • pire)—a large area ruled by one central government

equator(e • KWAY • ter)—an imaginary geographical line that divides the Northern Hemisphere from the Southern Hemisphere

expedition(ex • pi • DIH • shun)—a trip made to accomplish a specific goal

fertile(FUR • til)—capable of growing plants

native(NAY • tiv)—occurring originally in a certain place

navigator(NAV • ih • gay • ter)—a person who sails ships

rain forest(RAYN FOR • ist)—a tall forest that grows in a very warm and rainy climate

remote(re • MOHT)—faraway; hard to reach

settlement(SET • il • ment)—a new place where people settle

source(SORSS)—where something begins

strait(STRAYT)—a narrow body of water that joins two larger bodies of water

terrace(TAIR • iss)—a raised, flat area

tributary(TRIH • byoo • terry)—a river that joins a larger river

Western Hemisphere(WEST • ern HEM • iss • fear)—the western half of the earth

MAJOR COUNTRIES IN SOUTH AMERICA

Country	Date of Independence	Capital
Argentina	1816	Buenos Aires
Bolivia	1825	La Paz; Sucre
Brazil	1822	Brasília
Chile	1818	Santiago
Colombia	1819	Bogotá
Ecuador	1830	Quito
Falkland Islands (British dependency)		Stanley
French Guiana (Department of France)		Cayenne
Guyana	1966	Georgetown
Paraguay	1811	Asunción
Peru	1821	Lima
Suriname	1975	Paramaribo
Uruguay	1828	Montevideo
Venezuela	1830	Caracas

INDEX

About the author

D.V. Georges is a geophysicist in Houston, Texas. Dr. Georges attended Rice University, earning a masters degree in chemistry in 1975 and a doctorate in geophysics in 1978.